LET'S PLAY SPORTS!

Karate

by Kieran Downs

BELLWETHER MEDIA • MINNEAPOLIS, MN

Blastoff! Readers are carefully developed by literacy experts to build reading stamina and move students toward fluency by combining standards-based content with developmentally appropriate text.

Level 1 provides the most support through repetition of high-frequency words, light text, predictable sentence patterns, and strong visual support.

Level 2 offers early readers a bit more challenge through varied sentences, increased text load, and text-supportive special features.

Level 3 advances early-fluent readers toward fluency through increased text load, less reliance on photos, advancing concepts, longer sentences, and more complex special features.

★ **Blastoff! Universe**

Reading Level

Grade **K**

Grades **1–3**

Grade **4**

This edition first published in 2021 by Bellwether Media, Inc.

No part of this publication may be reproduced in whole or in part without written permission of the publisher. For information regarding permission, write to Bellwether Media, Inc., Attention: Permissions Department, 6012 Blue Circle Drive, Minnetonka, MN 55343.

Library of Congress Cataloging-in-Publication Data

Names: Downs, Kieran, author.
Title: Karate / by Kieran Downs.
Description: Minneapolis, MN : Bellwether Media, 2021. | Series: Blastoff! readers. Let's play sports! | Includes bibliographical references and index. | Audience: Ages 5-8 | Audience: Grades K-1 | Summary: "Relevant images match informative text in this introduction to karate. Intended for students in kindergarten through third grade"- Provided by publisher.
Identifiers: LCCN 2020029183 (print) | LCCN 2020029184 (ebook) | ISBN 9781644874257 (library binding) | ISBN 9781648341021 (ebook)
Subjects: LCSH: Karate–Juvenile literature.
Classification: LCC GV1114.3 .D68 2021 (print) | LCC GV1114.3 (ebook) | DDC 796.815/3–dc23
LC record available at https://lccn.loc.gov/2020029183
LC ebook record available at https://lccn.loc.gov/2020029184

Editor: Rebecca Sabelko   Designer: Josh Brink

Printed in the United States of America, North Mankato, MN.

Table of Contents

What Is Karate?

Karate is a **martial art**.
It teaches different hits.
It also teaches control.

Students train in **dojos**.

training in a dojo

This sport is most popular in Japan. But it is practiced around the world.

RYO KIYUNA

- **Kata**

- **Japan Karate Federation**

- **Accomplishments:**
  - **Gold medal winner at Karate World Championships 3 times**
  - **2017 gold medal winner at World Games**
  - **Gold medal winner at Asian Karate Championships 4 times**

Karate is now in the **Olympics**. It was added for the Tokyo Games.

What Are the Rules of Karate?

Karate has three main parts. **Kihon** teaches punches and kicks. It also teaches **blocks**.

A straight punch uses power from the whole body. A front kick is fast and strong.

KARATE MOVES

straight punch

front kick

upper
rising block

Students practice form and sets of movement in **Kata**. Each set mixes different moves.

practicing Kata

Students practice against pretend **foes**.

Kumite is **combat** training. It mixes moves and skills.

Students move freely. They practice moves on each other.

Kumite
training

13

Karate is judged in **competitions**.

Kata competition

Students are judged on
their moves in Kata events.
They earn points based on skill.

Kumite match

Kumite **matches** put two students against each other. They earn points for hits.

Whoever scores the
most points wins!

Students wear loose jackets and pants. Belts show their skill levels.

KARATE BELTS

white	beginner
yellow	
orange	
blue	
green	
purple	
brown	
black	advanced

Students practice with bare feet.

Students also use safety gear.

They wear pads on their hands and feet. These help to soften hits. **Kiai**!

pads

Glossary

blocks—movements that stop another person's attacks in karate

combat—referring to a fight between two people or groups

competitions—events in which someone tries to win something someone else is trying to win

dojos—places where martial arts are practiced

foes—enemies

Kata—a form of karate in which students practice an order of moves against pretend foes

kiai—a short shout yelled when doing an attack move

Kihon—the practice of the basic skills that are taught in karate

Kumite—a form of karate in which students practice a mix of moves and skills against other students

martial art—one of many forms of fighting and self-defense that are also practiced as sport

matches—contests between two or more individuals or teams

Olympics—related to the Olympic Games; the Olympic Games are worldwide summer or winter sports contests held in a different country every four years.

To Learn More

AT THE LIBRARY

Lacey, Saskia. *Spectacular Sports. Martial Arts.* Huntington Beach, Calif.: Teacher Created Materials, 2018.

Shaffer, Jody Jensen. *Who Is Jackie Chan?* New York, N.Y.: Penguin Workshop, 2020.

Wiseman, Blaine. *Martial Arts.* New York, N.Y.: AV2 by Weigl, 2018.

ON THE WEB

FACTSURFER

Factsurfer.com gives you a safe, fun way to find more information.

1. Go to www.factsurfer.com.

2. Enter "karate" into the search box and click 🔍.

3. Select your book cover to see a list of related content.

Index

The images in this book are reproduced through the courtesy of: Kaderov Andrii, front cover (hero); Studio MDF, front cover (background); 7stock, p. 4; Africa Studio, pp. 4-5; Chris Willson/ Alamy, p. 6; Nippon News/ Alamy, pp. 7, 20-21; Authentic Images, p. 8; Zoonar/Vladimir Galkin/ Alamy, p. 10; Hafizullahyatim, p. 11; A_Lesik, pp. 12, 16, 20; Yohei Osada/Aflo/ Alamy, pp. 12-13; Jorge Silva/ Alamy, pp. 14, 15; testing, p. 17; jasminko Ibrakovic, pp. 18-19; M.E. Mulder, p. 19.